Copyright 2024 Kimberley Hillis

All rights reserved. No part of this book my be reproduced, transmitted or stored in an information retrieval system in any form or by any means, graphic electronic or mechanical, including photocopying, taping and records, without prior permission from the publisher.

catastrophize [kəˈtæs.trə.faɪz]

verb

to think about the worst things that could possibly happen in a situation, or to consider a situation as much worse or much more serious than it really is

For Victoria and Edward

&

For L

This book is not intended to beat yourself over the head with every time you find yourself catastrophizing. This is meant to be used as a reminder that, even though it may feel like it, the worst outcome that you can imagine is just as likely not to happen.

Also, don't just use this book for those times that things work out flawlessly. Every time you've catastrophized an outcome, even if it's only worked out ok, (as opposed to perfectly) write that down for your reflection.

My greatest hope is in using this book, you will learn that, even if it doesn't feel like it in the moment, things will most of the time work out just fine. How do I know? That's up to you to document **your** real-life proof right here in these pages.

Kimberley xxx

Date: _____

The trigger: _____

_____
_____
_____
_____
_____

What I convinced myself would happen: _____

_____
_____
_____
_____
_____

How I was feeling:
- ☐ Anxious
- ☐ Frustrated
- ☐ Angry
- ☐ Helpless
- ☐ Hopeless
- ☐ Scared

I was lacking in:
- ☐ Sleep
- ☐ Food
- ☐ Fresh Air
- ☐ Sunlight
- ☐ Self-Care
- ☐ Boundaries

How it actually turned out:

What I wish I could have/would have thought from the start:

Additional thoughts:

Date: _____

The trigger: _____

_____
_____
_____
_____
_____

What I convinced myself would happen: _____

_____
_____
_____
_____
_____

How I was feeling: ☐ Anxious   ☐ Frustrated   ☐ Angry
                    ☐ Helpless   ☐ Hopeless   ☐ Scared

I was lacking in: ☐ Sleep   ☐ Food   ☐ Fresh Air
                    ☐ Sunlight   ☐ Self-Care   ☐ Boundaries

How it actually turned out:

_____
_____
_____
_____
_____
_____

What I wish I could have/would have thought from the start:

_____
_____
_____
_____

Additional thoughts:

_____
_____
_____
_____
_____

Date: _____

The trigger: _____

_____

_____

_____

_____

_____

What I convinced myself would happen: _____

_____

_____

_____

_____

_____

How I was feeling: ☐ Anxious   ☐ Frustrated   ☐ Angry
                     ☐ Helpless   ☐ Hopeless   ☐ Scared

I was lacking in: ☐ Sleep   ☐ Food   ☐ Fresh Air
                     ☐ Sunlight   ☐ Self-Care   ☐ Boundaries

How it actually turned out:

What I wish I could have/would have thought from the start:

Additional thoughts:

Date: _____

The trigger: _____

_____

_____

_____

_____

_____

What I convinced myself would happen: _____

_____

_____

_____

_____

_____

How I was feeling: ☐ Anxious   ☐ Frustrated   ☐ Angry
                    ☐ Helpless   ☐ Hopeless   ☐ Scared

I was lacking in: ☐ Sleep   ☐ Food   ☐ Fresh Air
                    ☐ Sunlight   ☐ Self-Care   ☐ Boundaries

How it actually turned out:

What I wish I could have/would have thought from the start:

Additional thoughts:

Date: _____

The trigger: _____

_____

_____

_____

_____

_____

What I convinced myself would happen: _____

_____

_____

_____

_____

_____

How I was feeling: ☐ Anxious ☐ Frustrated ☐ Angry
 ☐ Helpless ☐ Hopeless ☐ Scared

I was lacking in: ☐ Sleep ☐ Food ☐ Fresh Air
 ☐ Sunlight ☐ Self-Care ☐ Boundaries

How it actually turned out:

What I wish I could have/would have thought from the start:

Additional thoughts:

Date: _____

The trigger: _____

_____

_____

_____

_____

_____

What I convinced myself would happen: _____

_____

_____

_____

_____

_____

How I was feeling: ☐ Anxious   ☐ Frustrated   ☐ Angry
                       ☐ Helpless   ☐ Hopeless   ☐ Scared

I was lacking in: ☐ Sleep   ☐ Food   ☐ Fresh Air
                       ☐ Sunlight   ☐ Self-Care   ☐ Boundaries

How it actually turned out:

What I wish I could have/would have thought from the start:

Additional thoughts:

Date: _____

The trigger: _____

_____

_____

_____

_____

_____

What I convinced myself would happen: _____

_____

_____

_____

_____

_____

How I was feeling: ☐ Anxious   ☐ Frustrated   ☐ Angry
                    ☐ Helpless   ☐ Hopeless   ☐ Scared

I was lacking in: ☐ Sleep   ☐ Food   ☐ Fresh Air
                    ☐ Sunlight   ☐ Self-Care   ☐ Boundaries

How it actually turned out:

What I wish I could have/would have thought from the start:

Additional thoughts:

Date: _____

The trigger: _____

_____

_____

_____

_____

_____

_____

What I convinced myself would happen: _____

_____

_____

_____

_____

_____

_____

How I was feeling: ☐ Anxious   ☐ Frustrated   ☐ Angry
                    ☐ Helpless   ☐ Hopeless   ☐ Scared

I was lacking in: ☐ Sleep   ☐ Food   ☐ Fresh Air
                    ☐ Sunlight   ☐ Self-Care   ☐ Boundaries

How it actually turned out:

What I wish I could have/would have thought from the start:

Additional thoughts:

Date: _____

The trigger: _____

_____
_____
_____
_____
_____
_____

What I convinced myself would happen: _____

_____
_____
_____
_____
_____

How I was feeling: ☐ Anxious   ☐ Frustrated   ☐ Angry
                    ☐ Helpless   ☐ Hopeless   ☐ Scared

I was lacking in: ☐ Sleep   ☐ Food   ☐ Fresh Air
                    ☐ Sunlight   ☐ Self-Care   ☐ Boundaries

How it actually turned out:

What I wish I could have/would have thought from the start:

Additional thoughts:

Date: _____

The trigger: _____

_____

_____

_____

_____

_____

What I convinced myself would happen: _____

_____

_____

_____

_____

_____

How I was feeling: ☐ Anxious   ☐ Frustrated   ☐ Angry
                    ☐ Helpless   ☐ Hopeless   ☐ Scared

I was lacking in: ☐ Sleep   ☐ Food   ☐ Fresh Air
                    ☐ Sunlight   ☐ Self-Care   ☐ Boundaries

How it actually turned out:

What I wish I could have/would have thought from the start:

Additional thoughts:

Date: _____

The trigger: _____

_____

_____

_____

_____

_____

_____

What I convinced myself would happen: _____

_____

_____

_____

_____

_____

How I was feeling: ☐ Anxious   ☐ Frustrated   ☐ Angry
                    ☐ Helpless   ☐ Hopeless   ☐ Scared

I was lacking in: ☐ Sleep   ☐ Food   ☐ Fresh Air
                    ☐ Sunlight   ☐ Self-Care   ☐ Boundaries

How it actually turned out:

What I wish I could have/would have thought from the start:

Additional thoughts:

Date: _____

The trigger: _____

_____

_____

_____

_____

_____

What I convinced myself would happen: _____

_____

_____

_____

_____

How I was feeling: ☐ Anxious   ☐ Frustrated   ☐ Angry
                    ☐ Helpless ☐ Hopeless   ☐ Scared

I was lacking in: ☐ Sleep   ☐ Food   ☐ Fresh Air
                    ☐ Sunlight ☐ Self-Care   ☐ Boundaries

How it actually turned out:

What I wish I could have/would have thought from the start:

Additional thoughts:

Date: _____

The trigger: _____

_____

_____

_____

_____

_____

What I convinced myself would happen: _____

_____

_____

_____

_____

_____

How I was feeling: ☐ Anxious   ☐ Frustrated   ☐ Angry
                    ☐ Helpless   ☐ Hopeless   ☐ Scared

I was lacking in: ☐ Sleep   ☐ Food   ☐ Fresh Air
                    ☐ Sunlight   ☐ Self-Care   ☐ Boundaries

How it actually turned out:

What I wish I could have/would have thought from the start:

Additional thoughts:

Date: _____

The trigger: _____

_____

_____

_____

_____

_____

What I convinced myself would happen: _____

_____

_____

_____

_____

_____

How I was feeling: ☐ Anxious   ☐ Frustrated   ☐ Angry
                    ☐ Helpless   ☐ Hopeless   ☐ Scared

I was lacking in: ☐ Sleep   ☐ Food   ☐ Fresh Air
                    ☐ Sunlight   ☐ Self-Care   ☐ Boundaries

How it actually turned out:

What I wish I could have/would have thought from the start:

Additional thoughts:

Date: _____

The trigger: _____

_____
_____
_____
_____
_____
_____

What I convinced myself would happen: _____

_____
_____
_____
_____
_____
_____

How I was feeling:
- ☐ Anxious
- ☐ Helpless
- ☐ Frustrated
- ☐ Hopeless
- ☐ Angry
- ☐ Scared

I was lacking in:
- ☐ Sleep
- ☐ Sunlight
- ☐ Food
- ☐ Self-Care
- ☐ Fresh Air
- ☐ Boundaries

How it actually turned out:

What I wish I could have/would have thought from the start:

Additional thoughts:

Date: _____

The trigger: _____

_____
_____
_____
_____
_____

What I convinced myself would happen: _____

_____
_____
_____
_____
_____

How I was feeling: ☐ Anxious ☐ Frustrated ☐ Angry
☐ Helpless ☐ Hopeless ☐ Scared

I was lacking in: ☐ Sleep ☐ Food ☐ Fresh Air
☐ Sunlight ☐ Self-Care ☐ Boundaries

How it actually turned out:

What I wish I could have/would have thought from the start:

Additional thoughts:

Date: _____

The trigger: _____

_____

_____

_____

_____

_____

What I convinced myself would happen: _____

_____

_____

_____

_____

_____

How I was feeling:
- ☐ Anxious ☐ Frustrated ☐ Angry
- ☐ Helpless ☐ Hopeless ☐ Scared

I was lacking in:
- ☐ Sleep ☐ Food ☐ Fresh Air
- ☐ Sunlight ☐ Self-Care ☐ Boundaries

How it actually turned out:

_____
_____
_____
_____
_____
_____

What I wish I could have/would have thought from the start:

_____
_____
_____
_____

Additional thoughts:

_____
_____
_____
_____

Date: _____

The trigger: _____

_____

_____

_____

_____

_____

What I convinced myself would happen: _____

_____

_____

_____

_____

How I was feeling: ☐ Anxious   ☐ Frustrated   ☐ Angry
                     ☐ Helpless   ☐ Hopeless   ☐ Scared

I was lacking in: ☐ Sleep   ☐ Food   ☐ Fresh Air
                     ☐ Sunlight   ☐ Self-Care   ☐ Boundaries

How it actually turned out:

What I wish I could have/would have thought from the start:

Additional thoughts:

Date: _____

The trigger: _____

_____

_____

_____

_____

_____

What I convinced myself would happen: _____

_____

_____

_____

_____

_____

How I was feeling:
- ☐ Anxious   ☐ Frustrated   ☐ Angry
- ☐ Helpless ☐ Hopeless   ☐ Scared

I was lacking in:
- ☐ Sleep   ☐ Food   ☐ Fresh Air
- ☐ Sunlight ☐ Self-Care   ☐ Boundaries

How it actually turned out:

What I wish I could have/would have thought from the start:

Additional thoughts:

Date: _____

The trigger: _____

_____
_____
_____
_____
_____
_____

What I convinced myself would happen: _____

_____
_____
_____
_____
_____
_____

How I was feeling:
- ☐ Anxious
- ☐ Frustrated
- ☐ Angry
- ☐ Helpless
- ☐ Hopeless
- ☐ Scared

I was lacking in:
- ☐ Sleep
- ☐ Food
- ☐ Fresh Air
- ☐ Sunlight
- ☐ Self-Care
- ☐ Boundaries

How it actually turned out:

What I wish I could have/would have thought from the start:

Additional thoughts:

Date: _____

The trigger: _____

_____

_____

_____

_____

_____

_____

What I convinced myself would happen: _____

_____

_____

_____

_____

_____

How I was feeling: ☐ Anxious   ☐ Frustrated   ☐ Angry
                      ☐ Helpless   ☐ Hopeless   ☐ Scared

I was lacking in: ☐ Sleep   ☐ Food   ☐ Fresh Air
                      ☐ Sunlight   ☐ Self-Care   ☐ Boundaries

How it actually turned out:

What I wish I could have/would have thought from the start:

Additional thoughts:

Date: _____

The trigger: _____

_____
_____
_____
_____
_____
_____

What I convinced myself would happen: _____

_____
_____
_____
_____
_____

How I was feeling:
- ☐ Anxious
- ☐ Helpless
- ☐ Frustrated
- ☐ Hopeless
- ☐ Angry
- ☐ Scared

I was lacking in:
- ☐ Sleep
- ☐ Sunlight
- ☐ Food
- ☐ Self-Care
- ☐ Fresh Air
- ☐ Boundaries

How it actually turned out:

What I wish I could have/would have thought from the start:

Additional thoughts:

Date: _____

The trigger: _____

_____

_____

_____

_____

_____

_____

What I convinced myself would happen: _____

_____

_____

_____

_____

_____

How I was feeling: ☐ Anxious   ☐ Frustrated   ☐ Angry
                    ☐ Helpless   ☐ Hopeless   ☐ Scared

I was lacking in: ☐ Sleep   ☐ Food   ☐ Fresh Air
                    ☐ Sunlight   ☐ Self-Care   ☐ Boundaries

How it actually turned out:

What I wish I could have/would have thought from the start:

Additional thoughts:

Date: _____

The trigger: _____

_____

_____

_____

_____

_____

What I convinced myself would happen: _____

_____

_____

_____

_____

How I was feeling: ☐ Anxious   ☐ Frustrated   ☐ Angry
                    ☐ Helpless   ☐ Hopeless   ☐ Scared

I was lacking in: ☐ Sleep   ☐ Food   ☐ Fresh Air
                    ☐ Sunlight   ☐ Self-Care   ☐ Boundaries

How it actually turned out:

What I wish I could have/would have thought from the start:

Additional thoughts:

Date: _____

The trigger: _____

_____

_____

_____

_____

What I convinced myself would happen: _____

_____

_____

_____

_____

How I was feeling: ☐ Anxious   ☐ Frustrated   ☐ Angry
                    ☐ Helpless   ☐ Hopeless   ☐ Scared

I was lacking in: ☐ Sleep   ☐ Food   ☐ Fresh Air
                    ☐ Sunlight   ☐ Self-Care   ☐ Boundaries

How it actually turned out:

What I wish I could have/would have thought from the start:

Additional thoughts:

Date: _____

The trigger: _____

_____
_____
_____
_____
_____
_____

What I convinced myself would happen: _____

_____
_____
_____
_____
_____
_____

How I was feeling: ☐ Anxious   ☐ Frustrated   ☐ Angry
                     ☐ Helpless   ☐ Hopeless   ☐ Scared

I was lacking in: ☐ Sleep   ☐ Food   ☐ Fresh Air
                     ☐ Sunlight   ☐ Self-Care   ☐ Boundaries

How it actually turned out:

What I wish I could have/would have thought from the start:

Additional thoughts:

Date: _____

The trigger: _____

_____
_____
_____
_____
_____

What I convinced myself would happen: _____

_____
_____
_____
_____
_____

How I was feeling: ☐ Anxious   ☐ Frustrated   ☐ Angry
                    ☐ Helpless   ☐ Hopeless   ☐ Scared

I was lacking in: ☐ Sleep   ☐ Food   ☐ Fresh Air
                    ☐ Sunlight   ☐ Self-Care   ☐ Boundaries

How it actually turned out:

What I wish I could have/would have thought from the start:

Additional thoughts:

Date: _____

The trigger: _____

_____

_____

_____

_____

_____

What I convinced myself would happen: _____

_____

_____

_____

_____

_____

How I was feeling:
- [ ] Anxious
- [ ] Frustrated
- [ ] Angry
- [ ] Helpless
- [ ] Hopeless
- [ ] Scared

I was lacking in:
- [ ] Sleep
- [ ] Food
- [ ] Fresh Air
- [ ] Sunlight
- [ ] Self-Care
- [ ] Boundaries

How it actually turned out:

What I wish I could have/would have thought from the start:

Additional thoughts:

Date: _____

The trigger: _____

_____

_____

_____

_____

_____

_____

What I convinced myself would happen: _____

_____

_____

_____

_____

_____

_____

How I was feeling: ☐ Anxious   ☐ Frustrated   ☐ Angry
                     ☐ Helpless   ☐ Hopeless   ☐ Scared

I was lacking in: ☐ Sleep   ☐ Food   ☐ Fresh Air
                     ☐ Sunlight   ☐ Self-Care   ☐ Boundaries

How it actually turned out:

What I wish I could have/would have thought from the start:

Additional thoughts:

Date: _____

The trigger: _____

_____

_____

_____

_____

_____

What I convinced myself would happen: _____

_____

_____

_____

_____

_____

How I was feeling: ☐ Anxious   ☐ Frustrated   ☐ Angry
                              ☐ Helpless   ☐ Hopeless   ☐ Scared

I was lacking in: ☐ Sleep   ☐ Food   ☐ Fresh Air
                              ☐ Sunlight   ☐ Self-Care   ☐ Boundaries

How it actually turned out:

What I wish I could have/would have thought from the start:

Additional thoughts:

Date: _____

The trigger: _____

_____

_____

_____

_____

_____

What I convinced myself would happen: _____

_____

_____

_____

_____

_____

How I was feeling:
- ☐ Anxious ☐ Frustrated ☐ Angry
- ☐ Helpless ☐ Hopeless ☐ Scared

I was lacking in:
- ☐ Sleep ☐ Food ☐ Fresh Air
- ☐ Sunlight ☐ Self-Care ☐ Boundaries

How it actually turned out:

What I wish I could have/would have thought from the start:

Additional thoughts:

Date: _____

The trigger: _____

_____
_____
_____
_____
_____
_____

What I convinced myself would happen: _____

_____
_____
_____
_____
_____
_____

How I was feeling: ☐ Anxious   ☐ Frustrated   ☐ Angry
                    ☐ Helpless ☐ Hopeless   ☐ Scared

I was lacking in: ☐ Sleep   ☐ Food   ☐ Fresh Air
                    ☐ Sunlight ☐ Self-Care   ☐ Boundaries

How it actually turned out:

What I wish I could have/would have thought from the start:

Additional thoughts:

Date: _____

The trigger: _____

_____

_____

_____

_____

_____

What I convinced myself would happen: _____

_____

_____

_____

_____

_____

How I was feeling: ☐ Anxious   ☐ Frustrated   ☐ Angry
                     ☐ Helpless   ☐ Hopeless   ☐ Scared

I was lacking in: ☐ Sleep   ☐ Food   ☐ Fresh Air
                     ☐ Sunlight   ☐ Self-Care   ☐ Boundaries

How it actually turned out:

_____
_____
_____
_____
_____
_____

What I wish I could have/would have thought from the start:

_____
_____
_____
_____

Additional thoughts:

_____
_____
_____
_____

Date: _____

The trigger: _____

_____

_____

_____

_____

_____

What I convinced myself would happen: _____

_____

_____

_____

_____

_____

How I was feeling: ☐ Anxious   ☐ Frustrated   ☐ Angry
                    ☐ Helpless   ☐ Hopeless   ☐ Scared

I was lacking in: ☐ Sleep   ☐ Food   ☐ Fresh Air
                    ☐ Sunlight   ☐ Self-Care   ☐ Boundaries

How it actually turned out:

What I wish I could have/would have thought from the start:

Additional thoughts:

Date: _____

The trigger: _____

_____
_____
_____
_____
_____
_____

What I convinced myself would happen: _____

_____
_____
_____
_____
_____
_____

How I was feeling:
- ☐ Anxious   ☐ Frustrated   ☐ Angry
- ☐ Helpless ☐ Hopeless   ☐ Scared

I was lacking in:
- ☐ Sleep   ☐ Food   ☐ Fresh Air
- ☐ Sunlight ☐ Self-Care   ☐ Boundaries

How it actually turned out:

What I wish I could have/would have thought from the start:

Additional thoughts:

Date: _____

The trigger: _____

_____
_____
_____
_____
_____
_____

What I convinced myself would happen: _____

_____
_____
_____
_____
_____
_____

How I was feeling:
- ☐ Anxious   ☐ Frustrated   ☐ Angry
- ☐ Helpless ☐ Hopeless   ☐ Scared

I was lacking in:
- ☐ Sleep   ☐ Food   ☐ Fresh Air
- ☐ Sunlight ☐ Self-Care   ☐ Boundaries

How it actually turned out:

What I wish I could have/would have thought from the start:

Additional thoughts:

Date: _____

The trigger: _____

_____

_____

_____

_____

_____

What I convinced myself would happen: _____

_____

_____

_____

_____

_____

How I was feeling: ☐ Anxious   ☐ Frustrated   ☐ Angry
                     ☐ Helpless   ☐ Hopeless   ☐ Scared

I was lacking in: ☐ Sleep   ☐ Food   ☐ Fresh Air
                     ☐ Sunlight   ☐ Self-Care   ☐ Boundaries

How it actually turned out:

What I wish I could have/would have thought from the start:

Additional thoughts:

Date: _____

The trigger: _____

_____
_____
_____
_____
_____
_____

What I convinced myself would happen: _____

_____
_____
_____
_____
_____

How I was feeling: ☐ Anxious   ☐ Frustrated   ☐ Angry
                    ☐ Helpless   ☐ Hopeless   ☐ Scared

I was lacking in: ☐ Sleep   ☐ Food   ☐ Fresh Air
                    ☐ Sunlight   ☐ Self-Care   ☐ Boundaries

How it actually turned out:

What I wish I could have/would have thought from the start:

Additional thoughts:

Date: _____

The trigger: _____

_____

_____

_____

_____

_____

What I convinced myself would happen: _____

_____

_____

_____

_____

_____

How I was feeling: ☐ Anxious   ☐ Frustrated   ☐ Angry
                  ☐ Helpless   ☐ Hopeless   ☐ Scared

I was lacking in: ☐ Sleep   ☐ Food   ☐ Fresh Air
                 ☐ Sunlight   ☐ Self-Care   ☐ Boundaries

How it actually turned out:

What I wish I could have/would have thought from the start:

Additional thoughts:

Date: _____

The trigger: _____

_____
_____
_____
_____
_____

What I convinced myself would happen: _____

_____
_____
_____
_____
_____

How I was feeling:
- ☐ Anxious
- ☐ Helpless
- ☐ Frustrated
- ☐ Hopeless
- ☐ Angry
- ☐ Scared

I was lacking in:
- ☐ Sleep
- ☐ Sunlight
- ☐ Food
- ☐ Self-Care
- ☐ Fresh Air
- ☐ Boundaries

How it actually turned out:

What I wish I could have/would have thought from the start:

Additional thoughts:

Date: _____

The trigger: _____

_____

_____

_____

_____

_____

_____

What I convinced myself would happen: _____

_____

_____

_____

_____

_____

_____

How I was feeling: ☐ Anxious   ☐ Frustrated   ☐ Angry
                    ☐ Helpless   ☐ Hopeless   ☐ Scared

I was lacking in: ☐ Sleep   ☐ Food   ☐ Fresh Air
                    ☐ Sunlight   ☐ Self-Care   ☐ Boundaries

How it actually turned out:

_____

_____

_____

_____

_____

_____

What I wish I could have/would have thought from the start:

_____

_____

_____

_____

Additional thoughts:

_____

_____

_____

_____

Date: _____

The trigger: _____

_____

_____

_____

_____

_____

What I convinced myself would happen: _____

_____

_____

_____

_____

_____

How I was feeling:
- ☐ Anxious ☐ Frustrated ☐ Angry
- ☐ Helpless ☐ Hopeless ☐ Scared

I was lacking in:
- ☐ Sleep ☐ Food ☐ Fresh Air
- ☐ Sunlight ☐ Self-Care ☐ Boundaries

How it actually turned out:

What I wish I could have/would have thought from the start:

Additional thoughts:

Date: _____

The trigger: _____

_____
_____
_____
_____
_____

What I convinced myself would happen: _____

_____
_____
_____
_____
_____

How I was feeling:
- ☐ Anxious   ☐ Frustrated   ☐ Angry
- ☐ Helpless   ☐ Hopeless   ☐ Scared

I was lacking in:
- ☐ Sleep   ☐ Food   ☐ Fresh Air
- ☐ Sunlight   ☐ Self-Care   ☐ Boundaries

How it actually turned out:

What I wish I could have/would have thought from the start:

Additional thoughts:

Date: _____

The trigger: _____

_____
_____
_____
_____
_____
_____

What I convinced myself would happen: _____

_____
_____
_____
_____
_____
_____

How I was feeling: ☐ Anxious   ☐ Frustrated   ☐ Angry
                    ☐ Helpless   ☐ Hopeless   ☐ Scared

I was lacking in: ☐ Sleep   ☐ Food   ☐ Fresh Air
                    ☐ Sunlight   ☐ Self-Care   ☐ Boundaries

How it actually turned out:

What I wish I could have/would have thought from the start:

Additional thoughts:

Date: _____

The trigger: _____

_____

_____

_____

_____

_____

What I convinced myself would happen: _____

_____

_____

_____

_____

_____

How I was feeling:
- ☐ Anxious   ☐ Frustrated   ☐ Angry
- ☐ Helpless ☐ Hopeless   ☐ Scared

I was lacking in:
- ☐ Sleep   ☐ Food   ☐ Fresh Air
- ☐ Sunlight ☐ Self-Care   ☐ Boundaries

How it actually turned out:

What I wish I could have/would have thought from the start:

Additional thoughts:

Date: _____

The trigger: _____

_____

_____

_____

_____

_____

What I convinced myself would happen: _____

_____

_____

_____

_____

_____

How I was feeling: ☐ Anxious   ☐ Frustrated   ☐ Angry
                     ☐ Helpless   ☐ Hopeless   ☐ Scared

I was lacking in: ☐ Sleep   ☐ Food   ☐ Fresh Air
                     ☐ Sunlight   ☐ Self-Care   ☐ Boundaries

How it actually turned out:

What I wish I could have/would have thought from the start:

Additional thoughts:

Date: _____

The trigger: _____

_____

_____

_____

_____

_____

What I convinced myself would happen: _____

_____

_____

_____

_____

_____

How I was feeling: ☐ Anxious   ☐ Frustrated   ☐ Angry
                    ☐ Helpless ☐ Hopeless   ☐ Scared

I was lacking in: ☐ Sleep   ☐ Food   ☐ Fresh Air
                    ☐ Sunlight ☐ Self-Care   ☐ Boundaries

How it actually turned out:

What I wish I could have/would have thought from the start:

Additional thoughts:

Date: _____

The trigger: _____

_____

_____

_____

_____

_____

What I convinced myself would happen: _____

_____

_____

_____

_____

_____

How I was feeling: ☐ Anxious   ☐ Frustrated   ☐ Angry
                     ☐ Helpless   ☐ Hopeless   ☐ Scared

I was lacking in: ☐ Sleep   ☐ Food   ☐ Fresh Air
                     ☐ Sunlight   ☐ Self-Care   ☐ Boundaries

How it actually turned out:

What I wish I could have/would have thought from the start:

Additional thoughts: